## Sky

Children draw me a ribbon
On top of the page
        Look inside the pool
Even you can fly on your back

# Milking The Earth

*Poems by*
*Perie Longo*

John Daniel, Publisher
Santa Barbara
1986

"Cabo San Lucas, Mex." and "Little Sister" were first published in *Connexions*.
"Saving Daylight Three Days Before the Assassination of Indira G." was first
published in *Catharsis*. "Hawk" and "Heron" were first published in *Studia Mystica*.

Cover photo by Gene Armstrong
Typeset in Electra by Jim Cook
Santa Barbara, California

LIBRARY OF CONGRESS CATALOGING IN PUBLICATION DATA
Longo, Perie, 1940–
Milking the earth.
   I. Title
PS3562.0524M54 1986   811'.54   86-13497
ISBN 0-936784-14-8 (pbk)

Published by
JOHN DANIEL, PUBLISHER
Post Office Box 21922
Santa Barbara, California 93121

# Contents

## Cabo San Lucas, Mex.

This land is not for sleeping
after all it is the end point
where sea throws itself against
a totem cliff great enough
to fort any complaint
before moving out to the next shore
days away
tonight a harangue

I wince at each pitting
and each whine of air tearing
around adobe corners that intrude
on flesh angles
hair straightens
as cliff like I face the moon

This morning my nephew
was electrocuted reaching
into a box   died on the spot
but someone blew hard into him
only his middle toe where
sparks grounded is gone
he's back holding onto
babbling about light

Next door gringos throw
fireworks beer cans and
hot breath off the porch
we could break off here into
the black

No one would know
but the sea   the rock at the end
and of course the wind
stuffing us with sand
so we couldn't say anything
insignificant
moving out

## *Tracing The Moth Backwards*

Not knowing she had anything
to give the woman traced the
flutter of a moth perhaps
brought home from the grocery store
nested in flour
backwards to a plastic bag
where she had hidden
two years ago the wing of a red
shouldered hawk found
at the base of a white hydrangea
soaked by an early riser
on voting day

Knowing the sacredness of such
a gift the woman lifted the hawk
from the ground and continued
running so as not to stop
the pound of her heart
which ballooned when voters passing by
stuck out their tongues in horror
at the head with eyes still open
staring upward flopping from roadside
to roadside though its body rested
firm in her hands

She hid it in the woods
behind the condominiums
under a pine so the gardener
wouldn't throw it in the garbage
and later after voting returned
to bury it
sectioning off the wing
to help her when things got tough
though it didn't come off easily
She covered her eyes
with purple sage blossoms
before the first handfuls of earth

At first she hid the wing on the roof
to dry never catching who came
into power when the polls closed
and for a year or so moved it
from place to place
until maggots at the torn flesh
gave up after the lysol treatment

This woman who was gentle enough
tracing the moth backwards
remembered the hawk wing
stood on the swivel chair
lifted it off the shelf
unwound the wire fastener
and from the mouth of the bag leapt
a hundred flying things throwing
her to the ground

The wing rushed out stripped
of feathers a fan of lace-fine bones
that once carried the hawk
she tried to preserve high
above earth's ledges
this woman who didn't know
grew hot and heavy
limped to the kitchen
and threw it in the trash

Now she sits and thinks
about the wing rubbing her shoulder
how she could have returned it
to pine and sage
she could have but the fan of bone
became a hold for everything
forgotten and missed

## The Penance

Her mother always said she was
straight from heaven but she knew
better   knew to keep her mouth
shut like the others didn't
and got whipped with the ivory
handled hairbrush   didn't want
her flesh to snap like fireworks
that never quite made it
didn't want her mouth to swell
like a frog's throat in heat
she couldn't bear that brand

so people thought the cat
got her tongue when really it came
down to the jellybean she ate
one Easter morning   she didn't tell
liking the idea of being straight
from heaven so took communion anyway
sure hell would rise up
and gobble her by the toes
any minute for breaking   the fast

There she was age seven
already living the difference
between what is said and done
Stomach pains put her in the hospital
more than once where they pressed
and pumped   nothing ever came up
she even tried sticking fingers
down her throat
when no one was looking
but that jellybean   she couldn't
remember the flavor   wouldn't budge

Some say she ate rattles of a snake
the way she shook and bristled
when anyone crossed her path
Once her eyes bit a chunk
out of someone's throat
but really it came down to words
the priest spoke when she told him
about the jellybean years later

Child your only sin was thinking
it was one he forgave but she didn't
and never finished the ten Hail Mary's
he gave her for a penance
why words ran right through her
after that she took satisfaction
in thunderstorms and following her daddy
who never said much around the garden
learning to grow roses
without thorns though it took hours
of watering and rubbing the scars

11

## Untitled

When she was found in a thicket
of sea grass high on a shelf
set into the shale cliff that rose
from sand to hold the city
from privacy of sea birds
and other wildness

they were not sure why a smile
swept her face when it appeared
from her cracked lips
she had been there a long time
and as long as she was still
breathing though no more than
a feather without the suggestion
of a whisper they bore
her down gradually

you could almost hear
the cliff squeeze her out
as the rocks rolled they panted
in rhythm with the surf
though she weighed almost
nothing no more than the
air which barely stirred

When they unfastened what
bound a pale orange feather
black at the tip knife pointed
blew from beneath her shirt
a flicker's someone said
and there was a miniature scallop
formed as the hand of the sea
tinted the last breath of sun

Then too a brown pebble escaped
glossed maybe from the way
her heart beat against it
as they stood there fingering
her treasures wondering whether
she had fallen or climbed

her eyes opened and smile
diminishing she whispered
that one I found in the Las Cruces
dump helping a childhood friend
gather brass gun pellets
she was planning to melt down
into a bed   how long have I been
asleep

## After Lunch Looking At A Rose

What am I doing writing this poem
when I should be inside the rose
outside my window rolling in waves
of pink over green seas skies gone steel
perhaps thinking how can I begin
to compare

When finally writing as always hoped
how could you remember me drifting
in a desert of glances outside the restaurant
leafing through poems looking up every time
a shadow moved in I should be inside
the children

who write them begging mercy
not to read before their class
Finger points are sharper than thorns
on the glorious rose outside my window
and they are only nine years old
going on

I stand up demand a phone
when the waitress says are you waiting
for someone I call you answer who
Now the rose is swinging perhaps
that pink because it knows
nothing else

This is the third time in a row
I accuse understand much more than that
you explain I am not the only one everyone
is furious well that's one way I'll say yes
come now the rose is absolutely swelling
in the fog

No I say when you settle across
from me the waitress sidestepping
folders shouting help at my feet
you are only partially the reason
a great excuse to remember all those moments
I have felt defaced nothing is
more important

than the rose standing up pain
is so demanding we agree how arrogant
the experts who insist what hurts us and
what doesn't giving up is too easy
All right don't wear your jacket your shoes
your nice shirt catch a cold please don't
forget me

Some things can't be helped
all I want is to touch once more inside
my child's petal soft dimple and the poems
before we forget why we exist I will be
here as long as I last time to go
visit the rose which has
such patience

## Weekend Seven Ways

To Mother:

Just he and I went without
the children hiking through
wildflower mile after aromatic
mile slowly moving northeast
drinking snow water
crossing river winds so often
there was no difference
between leather and flow
until at dusk a coiled snake
scared me into rock
Leveled today
it is all right to do laundry
Fog cools everything
most wounds


To the Husband:

Promising destination worth
the push I led us up furnace ledges
down into dark rushings chanting
the moment's glory when guarding
the narrows sprung Queen Mother
hissing halt
Torn with whether to freeze
or flee I asked what to do
You jeered never reason
with an angry woman
The rock snapped and I limped
down trail after you again

16

To the Children:

I would want myself brave
for the prints I leave
in dust
some you are certain to see

Despite the hiking stick
you fashioned from bamboo
with native symbol
for courage
I darted like a mouse
from the feast
I ordered

Help me
my knee doesn't bend
the heart is another thing


To a Close Friend:

Unable to remember dreams
you spoke softly be awake for them
Looking up at stars thinking
of all the impossibles
paralyzed between fiery eyes
refusing passage I remembered
our wish for release of obstacle
knowing myself as snake


To the Medicine Man:

This snake rattling
teaches I have
a long way to go
before I deserve
to be where I am

To the Rattlesnake:

You sing
at my coming
Not understanding
I open my mouth
wrongly and shake
a stick

Poison message
no kits for that
no antidote
but silence
chasing chasing me
into darkness

Next time I will
sing back to
your tradition
and we will
both sleep


To Hokshida:

Leg braced I am propped
at the altar of longing
A fresh rose rattles its petals
Eagle wing walks on bone
We have set children dancing
at the zoo
Secured feathers in their hair

Not moving I hear us flying
learning to become old

## *stepping in*

in the backdrop
i listen to them all
ebbing in/out
of each other strings
toward/away     wailing/laughing
for the dead sister
mother wife daughter

i replace in the backdrop
humming aside/along
outbreaks/suspensions
tapping my foot
to the guitar's
pluck a plank
keeping up a little off

from their counterpoint
just managing to hum along
out of step
straining to assimilate
the pluck a plank
of their chords
and the drip a drop
of rain running down
out my side

## Beneath the Jacaranda Tree

Forty minutes to spare
purple bellows lead me
up a 3-D cliff replete
with toe notches
it was not so easy

shinnying up the drain pipe
of the family home
locked to burglars
when I was too young
to keep a key

Youngest and first
to arrive I always stole
the strongest whiff
of two-story high lilac
reaching the upper porch
where I sat Indian style
knowing a door would open
soon enough

With strong arms
and love of overview
I must climb to the top
of anything carrying paper
feign deafness
at come down
you'll fall cries
I answer like a crow
I'm too young
to keep a key

Forty years isn't long
to be in one place
awaiting entrance
only to learn I've been
inside the whole time

# Coming
# of
# Age

## Gopher Count Day:
## Viola County, Mn.

In glass jars farmers brought them
pickled
25¢ per pair of feet
killed
any way they could

I was sent out to pick thistles
from the pea patch
1¢ per stickler
hacked
any way I could

Dressed in leathers
sun at 98° softening me
on my belly
in a vine sea
I uprooted one enemy
and came eye to eye
with the other
up for air

panting

I let him go
never told anyone
collected $1 for thistles
and burrowed
into bed

the day the band broke forth
the day the grand marshall
rallied on a stallion
hung with gopher feet

the day they all
got drunk
and the crops grew

## Little Sister

I trained for the circus
stood on my head
until I blacked out
did backbends until I saw
earthworms rise between my feet

mastered ten cartwheels
in a row single handed
figuring I'd put Margaret O'Brien
out of business who I saw on film
walk a tightrope in tutu
and gallop bareback
on point

Big sisters trying to help
disciplined me into splits
until I cried Mama Mama
who scolded from her nap
leave her be
                    leave her be
                    they echoed
she's a late bloomer

For high jumping I won a ribbon
snapped some ribs thinking
I could break a stallion
under a tortilla moon
stuffed some pillows
beneath my waist
no money for a brace dreaming
some day I'd match up

I learned to push against walls
now can walk a tightrope
single handed back straight
and will stand on my head
at the snap of a finger
picking flowers from clouds
with my toes pointed

No one notices Mama
there's more than
three rings

## Of Fences and Buffalos

Ivy grows around me I am told
well what else
when you come from Wauwatosa
a square red brick house
on the corner set off
with a picket fence
I painted white every spring
then had to cut my hair
streaked from lack of skill
and looking up for help

I think about young Sioux
painted white made to stand
before charging buffalos
When they did not flinch
not one muscle anywhere
hunters poised behind for aim
welcomed them into the lodge
on a glass prairie lit with red
ivy grows around me

Though not young I am charged
it won't take long ten minutes
or so what did I mean
do not hide behind symbols
who do I think I am
in and out I paint the fence
turning white looking
around for help

At the bar people wait behind
I must not flinch anywhere
saying I cannot say
In the room where I lectured
is a circle of empty chairs
and party cups
I am God wrote a man
I'm sorry Mother wrote a woman
hunters fade

A buffalo in my mailbox
on a magazine ad announcing
a special offer welcomes me
I am from Wauwatosa the red house
on the corner with a white fence
I painted every spring
One summer my parents went to Europe
I painted the living room
chartreuse    well what else

## Coming of Age

There comes a time when
it is right to lace the hair
with wildflowers and breathe
burning herbs with the old ones
dance in bright flesh
under the moon teaching what it is
to be full and chiseled
and full again

There comes a time when
what is clung to is no longer useful
and releases itself like rain
arms spread in dream
for all to see what binds
is only ignorance of a fearsome lover
or shoes become too tight

and when the drum beats like thunder
that is the time to raise off earth
sure of its faithfulness
and give into the body
its fine hair feathering
sensing new landscape

Then is the time
to embrace all that is strange
announce your name as if
it has never been pronounced before
summon new robes and feasting

and stand erect for a crown
of woven grass from the hand
of a child reaching through
folds and folds of time

## Backstage

Brushing shades of brown
above roads of white on my face
to form wrinkles for the aged lady
I must play blends away thoughts
of you for awhile

I must concentrate the lines
be not too harsh nor soft
the bags beneath my eyes
just deep enough
and when the job is done

I look at me thirty years from now
horrified you are still there
pitying me through my own eyes
talking to me between my ears

*Places* is called
I bend into a stoop to fit my face
our eyes and hobble off
to play us out

## Masque

Paper shavings kneaded plastered
dried in the sun become a creature I
have never seen who tells me
we are all the same being
under different form

The river flows because it is
impossible to stay in one place
We stretch out so far we have to
re-enter ourselves where moss

has grown over brows grown heavy
with hair skin masks the lines
found in mountains risen when earth
cried oh no and sky answered take me
or I will disappear

As we age secrets become visible
Antlers grow where a halo tried
to shine finally we come to a clearing
in the forest no one knows who we are

because it is impossible to see
yourself staring back

No one knows what we mean anymore
because we mean everything and nothing
at the same time how can we sort it out
and most of all we learn to be
silent in the face of thunder

which is only the gods laughing
as we walk right past ourselves

## Toward Taos Without Camera

I was meant to have all of you
not just head of sky with hair
                    drifting
eye of passage between cliff profiles
shoulder of clay
arm of river
limb of shaking gold
leg of tree
foot of earth

You saw to it that when I came
you'd have me as you are
no
this is not the time for a camera
forgotten in the trunk
of someone's car

How will I prove you
with nothing between us
no format or lens

Closing tight over each other
horizons explode
I am in your continual eye
uneasy specks set
in your petrified breast

When I hold my camera again
I'll know what it is
to be unconcerned with proof

## Southern Belle

Sleeping in the guest room across
the redwood patio is a woman whose hand
I used to hold as we pulled my wagon
rusty red toward Saturday marketing
at the A & P fat red letters on white
right next to the ice rink we trudged
boots squeaking over the stuff angels
are made from when you lie down and sweep
legs & arms back & forth

Across the alley from the ten story
apartment building where we used to live
before we moved into the red brick house
on the corner in Wauwatosa two blocks
from the A & P and four blocks from the
bakery where we stopped on the way home
to buy Kugelhopf for Sunday breakfast
lived a mortician we called Angel Man
I liked because he smiled when bodies
arrived draped in white and I'd lie down
and rush my limbs back & forth imagining
they'd walk out his back door good as new

The woman in the guest room retired
early tonight after soaking her fractured
arm in the hot tub saying she felt good
as new despite the busy day we had I held
her arm so she wouldn't stumble as we went
sightseeing trudging back & forth up
the mission stairs white as snow remembering
my Father who died today
twelve years ago bells pealing noon
we knelt and lit a vigil candle red

This woman whose hand I used to hold
who washed the dishes tonight one arm
in a sling and watched my daughter
so I could hike up & down the mountain
asked if I could bring back a rock for her
since she was unable to climb
My father from the mountains where rocks
are rusty red and she from the South
once sliced open a thunder egg for me
mounted a sliver in silver finer than
any family heirloom I still wear around
my neck they used to call me Angel Girl

All I find is sandstone under dusk's red
clouds my father called ghost riders
fishing for rainbow trout in the mountains
she painted waiting for him she points out
a shell in my basket looks like a fish
I give her the whelk waving arms back & forth
after all she brought me Great-grandma's
silver wedding goblet with an angel girl stem
her paintings leap from the wall isn't it time
to go it's getting late tea in Grandma's
haviland waits getting cold

31

While my daughter performs gymnastics
before the TV broadcasting Olympic tumblers
tossing stuffed animals up & down from
her red wagon I promise my mother whose arm
suddenly flips from her sling and claps
her cheek that tomorrow we'll drive up
the mountain and fish for a rock red
as a ghost rider and watch sunset form
angels fat as the letters of the A & P

My father from the mountains is buried
in the southern flats where she was born
where they met and where we traveled
back & forth   Good as new my mother
whose hand I am privileged to hold again
swings through the back screen door
would I be an angel and find
her red sweater the night is cold

# Journey
## (To my Father)

I strapped a promise on my back
and packed into the canyon
switching back through years
each whittled with separate rage
limestone
        sandstone
                redstone
                        shale
and there the bridge suspended
hewn from longing I vowed
one day I'd cross some time

One time you built a well
for me sized to my hands
a wishing one
from lost mine diggings
we prodded from the earth
chips of limestone sandstone
redstone veined with fool's gold
                        teasing
you told me if I cast a coin
each day I'd have full life

Swinging across your river
always charging bearing down
into another climate
that well is mine again
and I admit hidden in grass
taller than old lies
I've had some life
am home
my feet sunk
in precambrian mud

## Mother's Day

Hey! Hey! Hey!
I would be could be flippant
but then read
"I lov you cuz your nis"
and arrange flowery weeds
just so picked from the field

Immemorialized
on rag paper smiling
at the washing machine
I tape up linear me where
I wouldn't hang Picasso
Ho! Ho! Ho!
and go to bed without washing
my face stick kissed

## *How Old I Am*
(for Joseph, age 6)

I am as old as one hundred minus
a few moons some so thin
you can hear them squeak
when clouds roll past
some fluffy as a croissant
I'd like to stuff with cheese
and eat so I could rise high
above your house
and slip a kiss of light
on your pillow for you to turn
upon when you're deep in dream

I am as old as the rings
of a bristlecone pine not finished
being around no matter how long
the winters
Every morning I am old
as the first peep of sun
and every night I am young
as a poem just born
looking for the warmth of your ear

## Birthday

A white teepee talks about
winter coming tightening slack
Poles shift casting me out
into sun so slight it hardly
knows shadows

From nowhere comes a dog
white fur thick enough
for both of us
We romp over earth mounds
tripping on chicken wire
laid flat to check slippage

come to an antique shop
where the owner honors
our sudden visit with
a pair of crude kachinas
a stranger just dropped off

Wood splinters fingers drawing
blood while the dog barks
I fly home in time to make
my son's birthday cake crying
before the batter hits the pan
love your sister
that's all there is

I give him a coin to spend
a rock to hold when he
doesn't know what to do
He holds me I know:
      remove splinters
      visit mother
      sit on earth
      bury the dog's bone
      move the teepee
from the mountain to my backyard
      catch my breath
      love my sister
      put the cake in the oven
      sing to my age
      and the slight sun
Snow falls somewhere
I light a fire

# April Fool's Day

The poem sticks
The lungs pump
I will live at least
for the next minute
long enough to practice death
tonight while the hamster escapes
rustling plastic behind
the sewing bureau
the cat forgets to lick
my face

The old man remembers
through tubes which suction fluid
thick with wintering
how he trucked melon pickers
back and forth across the border
the iron lung presses air in and out
a little longer
long enough to worry about
his money

Machines trace
the irregularity of the heart
he opens an eye
occasionally calling for his heirs
who remain absent

So many leave unannounced
I lead children to their own poems
just in case
when I was 8 they laughed at me
leaning on the school's chain link fence
writing myself into existence

A second grader writes God
is picking his nose
they laugh    I whisper
8 times 8 is more than enough
the screeching bell does not move them
poems wail off the walls
only one cloud consumes the sky
the old man dies

In a few days someone
will play the organ
someone will cry
God will sneeze and no one
will have a handkerchief

# Halloween Queen

She organizes spooks
telling them who they may
or may not scare
instructs on what pitch
and duration to sound their boos!

She orders skeletons about
specifying which closets
they may or may not inhabit
turning her nose up
at Mother's story of a stray one

She coaxes forth her cats
insisting they fast
through the day so they'll be
full voiced when it matters
securing spiders with globs
of tape on cotton roll webs

Professing witchness she tips
the brim of a black cone hat
to contact friends their eyes
owl sized following her sweep
around the yard where her broom
only occasionally touches ground

Though her brother says
she's cruel and rude for hiding
a lizard in his pillow case
she knows Halloween a safe vehicle
for her dark sovereignty
and when the wind arrives

She floats outside in a white gown
golden crown perched
precisely on a neat head
grinning with jiggly teeth
"treats please"
rendering monsters obsolete

## Up For Air

I watch my sons surf
chaff of hurricane
gliding on foam
shining in a stream
        of rain
burst from ocean seam
only their heads
above water

On land I surface
invisible

birth is so sudden

## Two Teachers Drumming

Together we drum beat
far off in your classroom
of turtles swimming mid air
we could be sitting
across the fire again
a skull in the sky
a bear of sun singing
while hawks dip toward
children's minds adrift
in the land of heart

Together we have nothing
left to say walls dissolve
the teaching pounds through
pencils splinters of tree
meaning of school to emerge
unite numbers light years
words make life happen
they become creatures of drum
minds of sound
knowing everything

while the next specialist
rolls in a keyboard
for a singing lesson
but already they have lifted
their voices instruments ancient
as this day meant to happen
our drums meant to meet
and beat together
we did we did
and the children listened

## *Walking The Red Brick Wall*

Dorothy I found your ruby shoes
in the lily pond at the bottom
where minnows sliver in and out
the toes
Dogwood and magnolia blossom
fly into green hands
holding down the water
risen where it doesn't belong
stealing cars gobbling houses
and there goes a body

A flag laughs red streams
A white arrow points opposite
from where I walk next to Grecian urns
ringed with maidens' heads
falling ferns aimed at the flash
of you I found beneath
the path of fish

There is nothing between us and the water
There is nothing under the grass
hungry for red brick
and wizards who carve roses out of metal
If I click my rubber heels together
perhaps we will come true

# Buying
# Time

## Buying Time

Check book balanced
on ledge
pen in hand
prepared to enter total
I wait as the cash register
itemizes
print-out lengthening
mesmerized as groceries
tumble over each other
like loose logs
in a rising river

The cashier asks if
I'm finished writing
clicks halt
lights buck
counters glare
muzak dies
I am totaled
and on my last check face
a poem

Efforts are whisked off
to cold storage
until I clear

# How The Freeways Came To Be

One year summer snapped on so suddenly
the sky became a mass of geese
hurrying north hissing and honking
with all that flapping of wings
the sky disappeared totally
people became frightened flying south
as fast as they could to where
air shouted blue and land swept gold

When they wrote home of the glory
relatives and friends soon came
oozing in great numbers of cars
hounding like dogs barking smoke
fat cars fast and black ones too

The hillsides confused called on
the rivers which flowed more generously
than ever crissing and crossing
bypassing range after range and
when the geese saw what had happened
they turned around to apologize
but no one looked up anymore
they just kept their eyes straight ahead

Troubled with the solid mass
with no heart the geese cried out
but no one heard anymore either
Mountains shrunk trees shook
rivers scattered every which way until
they lost their heads and turned to stone

Now people find it easier to roll
freely toward the sea over which
the geese still cry their sorrow
which falls as rain every winter
when they return to apologize

## Rain On Canvas

I am a circle unwinding
I am your heart undamned

Wings of sound come
to ground transparent thoughts

while your body disappears
with other breathless ones

I am the drum of sky beating
steady from the other side

uprooting that you may walk
where before it was impossible

How soft the earth now
hear yourself and ride me

wildly as far as
you must

## Halcyon Days

So too have I learned
gods give no reason why
they or we do what is done
but on a day such as this
of cool translucence
I see through love's demands

recognize people bobbing
beside each other
on a sea of blue leaves
and the architecture
of trees tapped robeless
on a gold sky

Hence my sigh casting
grief out on a string
which returns
in this windless state
with only end at end
a quill

Love's remains
are the reason for brushing
against myth against those
who give us something
from which to leap
a shore from which to fly

# Light Show

This place I come often
doesn't have a name
just a place stumbled upon
running one day loving
the loam beneath my feet

Then voices coming
the smell of horse
before that the special sound
of saddle idling over
slick hide I could tell
was brown from the thump
and sudden crack
"this here's a horse trail"

Something reared within
I grinned so glad I was
in the right place
being Sagittarius
The leader held reins taut
gathered me into heaving

I sidestepped into trillium
stumbled over logs here
to this place with no name
river fed from who knows where

Long after they left I
returned springing from
sunken hoof print to
hoof print and come here
often unsure of the next step

In shade decide to wade
to sun centered in the middle
of the week   remove shoes
roll jeans up   voices again

This time water swish
green silk   magpie and sun
shouting through leaves
rumbles light along branches
Everything pulses with nothing
I can touch and there are
more yellow flowers
than I can count

*Analyzing The Data*

(After the Challenger)

I open the door for the cat
who won't leave me alone
four dawns after the explosion
to grass gold singing high
in natal light and last week's
funny dream

       Computer break down...
       inside the disk insert
       7 white plastic astronauts
       bonded together pop up
       when I insert my finger
       and explode

Later    (time is a figure
of speech)    I invite children
into my dream gone haywire
on a blue sky screen people clawing
at the relentless dragon
whose scales and breath we ride

An unexpected letter arrives
from the teacher whose voice
rushes through waves to reach
for the stars a sock is retrieved
and a metal shoe that tried
to ground space

Analyzing
the
Data

Looking up we kicked a hole in the
grass which sings this morning
but there are no worksheets
for lessons that drift in from space
in the rain in the fire
in the wind in the sea

in the heart a new constellation
in the sky after smoke from
       the funny dream
           clears

## Saving Daylight Three Days Before
## The Assassination of Indira G.

Evenings work is cut out
Write to thank Mother for the
Happy Anniversary card and check
to celebrate sixteen years
(hands quickly fell off the watch
I gave)    and thank sister for
nephew's wedding photos (white/rose
color scheme carried out over
raked lawns) complete unemployment
forms (suddenly my job disappeared)
fill out form to qualify for visiting
Indians in prison    balance checkbook
put out old clothes (suddenly outgrown)
call friend who has a growth
denser than cyst
set back the clock

(suddenly making no difference)
Last night I heard the XIVth Dalai Lama
say love your enemy in the gym
a #8 hanging above his head along with
a sign THE FIELD HOUSE: CENTER
FOR FINE SPORTSWEAR    play ball
play war in the right clothes
His Holiness in gold/maroon robes
picks up a pink rose at his feet
where a beautifully arranged woman
in white left it    he coughs
places it in a vase of precise marigolds
Enemies build strength of character
the rose slips    monks bow
why did you leave Tibet someone asks
the Ocean of Wisdom says hmmmmmmm
it was no longer useful

Smile at your enemies
who suffer as well it's that simple
John from England who wears Birkenstocks
drives for the Dalai and calls ahead
making arrangements suddenly quit his job
and is leaving for India
We all stand and bow at the Lama
who rearranges his robes casting a smile
Today I heard Thomas B. spokesman
for the Hopi instruct meditate
fast   watch the grass grow to stop
the prophecy a gourd of insidious ash
showering over the earth
I tell Thomas wearing turquoise beads
over a flannel shirt with a red scarf
tied around his head the Dalai L.
says the same thing
He says hmmm and smiles

Tonight my daughter whose pajamas
are on inside out asks why mommies
always say hummmm when they are asked
questions and laughs when I say hmmmmmmmm
stroking white/rose wedding pictures
sinking into gold/maroon leaves
I remove turquoise beads
put on my flannel nightgown outside in
and set back the clock
my work cut out   tomorrow
there are pumpkins to be carved

# Mayday

Peaches on the tree are turning
along with everything else
even women's skirts in Kiev
on a perfectly normal day a voice
dry as dust announces
there is the sun dancing on the river
the seabird flying as usual
nothing is the matter be calm
notice the white teeth of the dancing women
flowers bright in their hair
skin falls from faces as I cut the chicken
into bite size pieces for family stew
evening news drones
only two dead today why do we cut
our lives into such tiny pieces

Sun the voice drones far more
dangerous than the cloud becoming
safer as it approaches unseen begins
to set except it never really does
we just turn away
ignore the obvious pretend calm
not cry fading something in me resists
hold me just once look deep
into the eye where you are inside a nucleus
a black hole and give me the news
nothing is the matter a doctor
from here will travel to Kiev
perform bone transplants for those
hidden behind the turning skirts that blur
with the truth it will take years
to talley the toll let's dance

well why not on this perfect day
normal in every way why not rhyme
there's no reason no sense no time
to waste lovers stroll across the avenue
the air waves then stop
to kiss to hold long stalling
traffic over here over there horns blaring
for different reasons with
geiger counters click clicking only
slightly above normal here we are safe
what we give comes back
what we take comes back
click click watch the birdy

Today I almost did a friend says
over the phone I stir the stew
words blur did what I ask not did
*died* almost did today take my life
but why the peaches
are turning and the sun never sets
honestly I report being calm perfectly
normal along with everything else
that's nice she says I pause
tell her today I turned over a friend
in the hospital with three verterbrae
crushed by a sloppy driver who hit and
ran horns blared no one stopped
no witness but her child of two
strapped in the back seat only able
to cry mama she crawled to him
her back broken they said it was a miracle
she lived so when she asked me
to turn her just roll the blanket
beneath her I was so afraid

but she wasn't is determined her bones
will mend by summer it's best to wait
wait until you feel really good if you
have the chance to decide anything
there's no time to waste
maybe our lives aren't our own
maybe we begin where we end
only a week ago I told an old man
NO crushing ants marching on spilled sugar
smashing them with his four footed cane
*scientists have proved what ants do*
*over here matters to those over there*
and I pointed up in the air about where
all the trouble is and saw a single leaf
on a branch spinning but he spoke
a language I did not understand
echoed *no no* and continued

Maybe I've gone on too long
my friend laughs like the women dancing
in Kiev I can almost see her teeth
maybe big brother is the fear the threat
the key pay attention
I love you we hang up the announcer
is still going on reports calmly
a tsunami threatens the stew burns
nobody eats my stomach turns but
I leave for the theatre anyway
which stands right next to the sea
everyone is there no one seems to mind
I am told to speak louder and eat
so much air the button on my skirt
explodes this may be my last chance
NO I pull myself together looking
into a mirror black as the lens
of your eye we must learn to whisper
in the dark and feel the similarity
of our bones this day

## *Eden*

This distance serves us well
To explore breadth of breath
Depth of longing

With something missing
This distance is
A holy place to fill
With grace and daring

Think of ice and sand
Soul and flesh
The distance between
Winter leaf and bud
Apart together

This distance bonds us
To dream—only far away
As a thought or God
Not just here
Flaming eternal

# Milking
# the
# Earth

## Milking The Earth
(For Nan and Bob)

Somewhere beneath dam waters
standing stiff in the sun
earth still remembers when creeks
wandered in silver ribbons one for
each fisherman and how
a simple clod was honored for its part
in the harvest

It remembers mud on polished
hearths and the pound of a heart
hooked up only to the eye which needed
no measure to see the stand of corn
had outdone itself
by the Fourth of July

and how proud the woman in a muslin
apron on Labor Day as she picked
from her hand set garden
a tomato trying its best to be
a pumpkin    her tears taken by sun

which barely matters to the dinosaur
stalking over the land its brain
tinier than all others wired to
control boards crying with greed
inside a mouth with no face

These things turn over in the mind
setting foot on earth of old
and the chair on the porch remembering
the body of the man who figured
for himself creaks in rhythm
to the wind which will never be
ploughed under run over

even as the perfect food
in the hot house listens
for the first breath of a
white eyed foal bound to beat
its story into some plot of ground

## Heron

Blue heron posing at slough edge
stalks burn-off rising in bellows
up over a eucalyptus break

its head jerking as if struck
with secrets easing up
from swamp bottom

I follow smoky spirals
with squinted eyes hoping to see
or hear what it does

There is only utter still
immobile for a solid second
I must capture on film

With camera ready for focus
the burn-off shoots out of frame
like a jet
        pulling the heron with it

leaving me posing at slough edge
with nothing on the other side
of my lens except my last breath
                        tailing after

## Hawk

You move us past
hills of resistance
to where land is supple
porous with movement
of speckled air through it

We rise and fall easily
over knolls breathing in
gentle voices of willow
and watching cow

Night moves in under rose
earth jumps up to touch
sun's final blaze and already
we see roads beneath us

ones traveled
dotted with headlights
winding into nothing
but a criss cross
of cricket talk

## Passing The Egret
(For Kathy)

Crowned with sky
jeweled with assurance
of its regal stance the egret
                    dips its beak
into marsh green haze
and you slip
between plump fingers
of a child
feeding you
her dreams
when you want
to run with
your own
black eyes
coursing
through
a heart silenced
too long
remarking
words
cannot possibly justice
such beauty

As the white figure lifts swiftly
at the edge of where our glance drops
lithe neck curving on the same air
that turns our cheeks red
I attempt glissade
thinking how quickly morning moves us
away from perfection

At least we made it to the bridge
                    and back
to a room full of white paper wings
and a long neck
of sudden light

behind lace curtains
casting shadows on respected wood

## The Condor

Why do you want me so much?
Is it that I am almost gone
or that you have not managed
to keep your eye on me

Long enough I will fly from Sisquoc
my head snapping fire speaking
from my crane hooked beak
I'm ugly in case you have forgotten
you who cry for beauty and peace
I am a buzzard unable to kill
if I could so many more
would have their dreams

Let me tell you I am past
cannot be reinvented
You have your satellites now
Those few of us left do not mind
our time has come we only
remind as you climb
craggy cliffs to rescue us
what happens when the once sacred
becomes a simple curiosity

On my underside is a white kite
and while you have been looking
for something beyond
stored me in a file the thread
has snapped in the wind

I want none of your pity
not I nor my unborn

Leave me in peace
One day I will return
looking for you

## Owl Feather Message

An owl slipped me into a spring
of grass to call you away from
ordinary things    to recall
far flights made close
to your heart

It wanted you to know the sky
is not as far away as you think
You're never alone as you feel
on this earth
speckled with your running
striped with your laughter
shaped by your thought

An owl left me as gift
to help you see through the dark
from all directions
and now you hold me
it wants you to remember

# *Waterfall*

The waterfall calls me
to jump from myself
the only way to remain
on the earth humming
with flight and rocks
crying what it is to be
still enough to hear
what trust means

The waterfall calls me
to the rainbow of bones
under earth tells me what
happened to lightning when
it struck why flowers shoot
flames crying when light
gets loose we will fall
like water which calls me

back to the mountain top
where my breath turned to snow
falling to earth which returns
to me again this spring rising
under splashes of my own doing
eyes green overtaking the trail
which led me here
to the water calling

returning to ash is only
the first step

## Gathering   What Is

dragonfly
            visits
waterfall    pool
      whirling with spider
                  dance
                  joins people
passing bread and song
                  lights
on the toes of a woman
      holding
                  very still
only shadows stir
      and from the way
            dead leaves move
                  snakes


woman
                  penetrates
liquid with fingers
water talks     rings around
                  the mind
                  wind picks up
carries people off
      clouds drift in    soon
firemaker will help
                  everything
                  sacrifice itself
and grow back
      except rocks which hold
            very still keeping
quiet
            no matter
                  what

## Reprieve

Sunny in the fog
yellow cream cup of morning
retaining dew from darkness
in your fragile curl
you pull glory
from my far reaches
expand that I may bury
my face in yours

Harshness at my elbow
will not tear at me
so easily now I lie
at your feet
already covered
with spring's dried burrs
waiting for the buzzing
to send me further
into the woods
deeper up river